BY COMMAND OF **His late Majesty** WILLIAM THE IVth.

and under the Patronage of

Her Majesty the Queen.

HISTORICAL RECORDS,

OF THE

British Army

Comprising the

History of every Regiment,

IN HER MAJESTY'S SERVICE.

By Richard Cannon Esqr.

Adjutant Generals Office, Horse Guards.

London.

Printed by Authority.

HISTORICAL RECORD

OF

THE MARINE CORPS,

CONTAINING

AN ACCOUNT OF THEIR FORMATION AND SERVICES FROM 1664 TO 1748;

AT WHICH PERIOD THOSE CORPS CEASED TO FORM PART OF THE ESTABLISHMENT OF THE REGULAR ARMY.

FROM THE YEAR 1755

THE PRESENT CORPS OF

ROYAL MARINES

HAVE BEEN UNDER THE CONTROL OF

THE LORDS COMMISSIONERS OF THE ADMIRALTY.

COMPILED BY

RICHARD CANNON, Esq.,

ADJUTANT-GENERAL'S OFFICE, HORSE-GUARDS.

The Naval & Military Press Ltd

Published by

The Naval & Military Press Ltd
Unit 10 Ridgewood Industrial Park,
Uckfield, East Sussex,
TN22 5QE England

Tel: +44 (0) 1825 749494
Fax: +44 (0) 1825 765701

www.naval-military-press.com
www.military-genealogy.com
www.militarymaproom.com

In reprinting in facsimile from the original, any imperfections are inevitably reproduced and the quality may fall short of modern type and cartographic standards.

THE MARINE REGIMENTS.

CONTENTS

OF THE

RECORDS OF THE MARINE CORPS.

Year		Page
	INTRODUCTION.	
1664	Formation of a Corps for Sea-service on commencement of war with Holland . .	1
——	Designated "*The Admiral's Maritime Regiment,* and commanded by the Duke of York, afterwards King James II. . . .	–
1672	Formation of additional Corps of Marines on renewal of hostilities with Holland . .	2
1689	*The Admiral's Maritime Regiment* incorporated in the Second Foot-Guards . . .	–
1702	Formation of six Regiments of Marines . .	–
——	Six other Regiments of Infantry selected for Sea-service	–
——	The Royal Warrant for forming the six Regiments of Marines, and for selecting six other Regiments for Sea-service . . .	3
——	Other Regiments embarked, at different periods during the war, to serve as Marines on board the Fleet	–
——	Rules and Instructions for the duties, pay, and clothing of the Marine forces . .	4

A 2

xxvi   CONTENTS OF THE RECORDS

Year		Page
1702	Placed under the control of the Lord High Admiral, the Prince George of Denmark	4
——	Appointment of Brigadier-General W. Seymour, of the Fourth Foot, to superintend the details of the Marine Regiments	5
——	Uniform prescribed for the Marine forces	—
——	Independent Companies of Marines formed for the fleet in the West Indies	—
——	Services of the Marines on board the fleet in the Mediterranean	—
1704	Proceeded in the fleet to Lisbon, to aid the cause of the Archduke Charles of Austria	—
——	Proceeded against Barcelona, but afterwards withdrew, and re-embarked	6
——	Attack and Capture of Gibraltar	—
——	Engagement of the British and French fleets in the Mediterranean	7
——	Siege of Gibraltar by the Spaniards and French	8
1705	The attempt to retake the fortress abandoned after a siege of seven months	9
——	The Marine Corps distributed in the several ships of war on the coast of Spain	10
——	Proceeded against Barcelona with the troops under the Earl of Peterborough	—
——	Capture of Fort Montjuich by storm	11
——	Surrender of the garrison of Barcelona	12
1706	Siege of Barcelona by the French	13
——	The French raised the siege and retreated	—
——	Capture of Carthagena	—
——	Capture of Alicant	14
——	Surrender of Iviça	—
——	Surrender of Majorca	—
1707	Attack and siege of Toulon	15
——	The siege of Toulon raised	—
1708	Surrender of Sardinia	—

OF THE MARINE CORPS. xxvii

YEAR		PAGE
1708	Capture of the Island of Minorca . . .	16
——	Decease of H. R. H. the Prince George of Denmark, Consort of Queen Anne, and Lord High Admiral of England	—
1709	Capture of *Anna-polis Royal*, in Nova Scotia .	17
——	Surrender of Alicant to the forces of Spain and France	—
1710	Capture of the Isle of Cette	18
——	The Isle of Cette recaptured . . .	—
1711	Proceeded on an Expedition against Quebec, in Canada	—
——	Failure of the expedition by storms and wreck in the River St. Lawrence	19
——	Decease of Joseph I., Emperor of Austria .	—
——	Election of Charles III. of Spain to be Emperor of Germany	—
1712	Negotiations for general peace . . .	—
1713	Definitive treaty of peace at Utrecht on 31st March	20
——	Gibraltar, Minorca, and Nova Scotia ceded to Great Britain by the treaty of peace . .	—
——	The Corps of Marines disbanded . . .	—
1714	Decease of Her Majesty Queen Anne on the 1st of August	—
——	Accession of King George I. . . .	—
——	Attempts of the Son of the late King James II to obtain the throne, defeated . . .	—
——	Augmentations made to the Army . .	21
——	Three of the late regiments of Marines, now the 30th, 31st, and 32nd, retained, and placed on the establishment of the infantry of the Line	—
1739	War declared against Spain on the 23rd of October, 1739	—
——	Augmentation of the Land forces . .	22

A 3

Year		Page
1739	Formation of six regiments of Marines	22
——	Fleet of five ships, with a detachment of Marines, under Admiral Vernon, proceeded against *Porto-Bello*	—
1740	An additional regiment of Marines, of four battalions, formed at New York in North America, and Colonel Spotswood appointed Colonel-Commandant	23
——	The six regiments of Marines augmented from 700 to 1000 men each	—
——	Augmentation of the four invalid companies of Marines	—
——	Usefulness of Marine forces, as proved on former occasions, now generally admitted	24
——	Formation of four additional regiments of Marines, of 1000 men each	—
——	Attack and capture of Fort Chagre	25
——	Fleet under Admiral Sir Chaloner Ogle, and troops, including the six Marine regiments under General Lord Cathcart, proceeded to the West Indies, for the purpose of attacking the Spanish possessions in South America	—
——	Death of General Lord Cathcart at Dominica	26
——	Brigadier-General Wentworth succeeded to the military command of the expedition	—
1741	The whole collected at Jamaica under Admiral Vernon	—
——	Proceeded to the *Grande Playa*, to windward of the town of Carthagena	—
——	Capture of forts *St. Jago* and *St. Philip*	—
——	Capture of the castle of *Bocca Chica*	27
——	Capture of Fort *St. Joseph*	—
——	Capture of the castle of *Grande Castello*	—
——	Attack of St. Lazar by escalade	—

Year		Page
1741	Repulse of the troops, and abandonment of the enterprise	28
——	The forts and castle of Carthagena demolished	—
——	The expedition returned to Jamaica	—
——	Another expedition proceeded to the island of Cuba	29
——	Returned to Jamaica after encountering much sickness and numerous casualties	30
1742	The island of *Rattan,* in the bay of Honduras, taken possession of, and placed in a state of defence	31
——	A detachment sent to the assistance of General Oglethorpe, in South Carolina, against the Spaniards	32
——	Recal of Admiral Vernon and General Wentworth	—
——	The independent Companies at Jamaica (now the Forty-ninth regiment) and the Marines on board of the fleet, completed with effective men; the remainder of the troops returned to England	—
——	The command of the fleet in the West Indies devolved on Sir Chaloner Ogle	—
1743	Another expedition proceeded to South America, under the command of Commodore Knowles of the Navy, with 400 men of the Thirty-eighth regiment and 600 Marines	33
——	Sailed to Antigua, and proceeded to attack La Guira in Terra Firma	—
——	Proceeded to Curaçoa to refit	—
——	Sailed again for Porto Cavallo	—
——	Attack of Ponta Brava	—
——	Returned to Jamaica	34
——	Declaration of war against France on 31st March, 1743	35

Year		Page
1744	Engagement of a party of Marines of the Essex ship-of-war in the Mediterranean	35
——	Active means adopted for completing the ten regiments of Marines	—
1745	Expedition against Cape Breton	36
——	Capitulation of Louisburg and of the Island of Cape Breton	—
1746	Complaints investigated respecting the settlement of accounts in the corps of Marines	37
——	Contemplated expedition against Quebec	38
——	Expedition proceeded against *Port L' Orient*	—
——	Disembarked in Quimperlay Bay, and advanced against Plymeur	—
——	Re-embarked and sailed for Quiberon	—
——	Returned to England	39
1747	Royal Warrant issued on the 28th February, 1747, for placing the Marine Forces under the control of the Lords Commissioners of the Admiralty	—
——	Renewed efforts of the King of France against the British possessions in North America, and in the East Indies	40
——	Victory over the French Fleet by Vice-Admiral Lord Anson and Rear-Admiral Sir Peter Warren, K.B., on the 3rd of May, 1747	41
——	Another victory over the French Fleet, by Commodore Fox, in June 1747	42
——	A further victory obtained on the 14th of October, 1747, by Admiral Sir Edward Hawke, over the French Fleet	—
1748	A fleet proceeded under Admiral Boscawen, with Marines and other troops, to attack the *Mauritius*	43
——	Proceeded thence to the *coast of Coromandel*	—
——	Disembarked and marched towards *Pondicherry*	44

Year		Page
1748	Obtained possession of *Arian Coupan* . .	44
——	Re-embarked after having demolished the fort of Arian Coupan	—
——	Another expedition, under Rear-Admiral Knowles, proceeded against St. Jago in Cuba	45
——	Squadron returned to Jamaica . . .	—
——	The King of France expressed a desire for Peace	—
——	Definitive treaty of Peace concluded at Aix-la-Chapelle on 18th October, 1748 . .	46
——	The ten regiments of Marines disbanded in November, 1748	—
1755	Preparations for renewing war with France .	—
——	Re-formation of the present Corps of Marines	—
——	Augmentations made in the Army and Navy .	—
——	Fifty Companies of Marines, formed in Three Divisions, raised under the control of the Lords Commissioners of the Admiralty . .	—
——	An Act of Parliament for the regulation of the Marine Forces while doing duty on Shore .	—
1802	The Royal Authority granted for the Marine Forces to be styled " *The Royal Marines* " .	47
1805	A *Fourth* Division formed at Woolwich by Order in Council dated 15th August 1805 . .	—
1827	Presentation of Colours, on the part of His Majesty King George IV., by His Royal Highness the Duke of Clarence, then Lord High Admiral, and afterwards King William IV.	48

PLATES.

Costume of Marines in 1742 .	. *to face Page*	1
Present Colours of the Royal Marines .	,,	48

CONTENTS

OF THE

APPENDIX TO THE MARINE CORPS.

YEAR		PAGE
	Authorities were granted by King William III. in 1694; by Queen Anne in 1713; and by King George I. in 1715, for deciding the Rank and Precedence of the Regiments of Infantry, and for giving Numeral Titles to the several Regiments, according to the dates of formation, or of being placed on the English establishment; as recommended by Boards of General Officers, at the several periods stated:—These regulations were confirmed by the Warrants of King George II., dated 1st July, 1751, and of King George III., dated 19th December, 1768	49
1660	The Regiments of Infantry, exclusive of the Three regiments of Foot-Guards, from the period of the Restoration of King Charles II., in 1660, to 1684, consisted of—	

The 1st, or the Royal Regiment.
The 2nd, or the Queen's Royal (First Tangier) Regiment.
The 3rd, or the Holland Regiment.
The 4th, (the Second Tangier) Regiment.

1685 The 5th and 6th Regiments were formed in Holland, in the year 1674, and were brought to England on the requisition of King James II., in 1685,—from which period they were authorized to take rank in the English Army—

CONTENTS OF APPENDIX TO MARINE CORPS.

YEAR		PAGE
1685	The Regiments of Infantry formed during the reign of King James II., and placed on the establishment of the army, were—	
	From 7th Royal Fusiliers to 17th Regiment	49
1688 and	During the reign of King William III.: From 18th Regiment to 27th Regiment	—
1689	The 18th Royal Irish Regiment was formed in Ireland in 1684; and the 21st Royal North British Fusiliers in Scotland in 1678: They were placed on the English establishment, the 18th in 1688, and the 21st in 1689, from which periods their numerical rank took effect	—
1702	Formed during the reign of Queen Anne:	
	From 28th Regiment to 39th Regiment	—
1717	Formed during the reign of King George I.:	
	From 40th Regiment to 41st Regiment	—
1739	Formed during the reign of King George II.:	
	From 42nd Regiment to 70th Regiment	50
And		
	The Marine Corps	52
1775	Formed during the reign of King George III.:	
	From 71st Regiment to 93rd Regiment	54
1793	The Scots Brigade brought from Holland	55
1800	The Rifle Brigade originally formed	—
1824	Formed during the reign of King George IV.:	
	From 94th Regiment to 99th Regiment	—

MARINES. 1742.
FOR CANNON'S MILITARY RECORDS

FORMATION AND SERVICES

OF THE

MARINE CORPS.

THE advantages arising from the services of corps trained to the use of arms *on board of ship, as well as on land,* were found when the British navy acquired a superiority over that of other nations of Europe; and as the safety of Great Britain, from its insular position, chiefly depends on the efficiency and excellence of her fleets, the importance and value of *Marine Forces* have consequently been at all times acknowledged and appreciated by the Sovereign, as well as by the Nation at large.

The first corps raised for Sea-service, of which history gives an account, is that which was formed by King Charles II., in the year 1664, when the war with Holland took place: this corps was commanded by the Duke of York (afterwards King James II.), then Lord High Admiral of Great Britain, and was designated "*The Admiral's Maritime Regiment.*"*

1664

---

* By Order in Council, dated 26th October, 1664, it was directed, that twelve hundred land-soldiers should be raised, in order to be in readiness for distribution in His Majesty's fleets; the whole to form one regiment, of six companies, under a Colonel, with a Lieutenant-Colonel, and Serjeant-Major; each company consisted of two hundred soldiers, with a captain, lieutenant, ensign, drummer, four serjeants, and four corporals. The regiment was armed with firelocks.

A subsequent Order in Council, dated 1st April, 1668, authorised the drawing of such numbers of soldiers from the Foot Guards, for His Majesty's service at sea, during the summer, as the Lord High Admiral might require.

2 FORMATION AND SERVICES OF MARINE CORPS.

1672 — In the year 1672 a dispute on the subject of naval precedence, and other causes, gave rise to another war with the Dutch, and battalions for *Sea-service* were formed, as the occasions of the State required, by drafts from the land-forces, which were embarked on board the fleet; several companies of the Foot Guards were employed on the Marine duty; these companies were engaged in a sharp fight with the Dutch fleet on the 28th of May, 1672, in which upwards of two thousand men were killed; they were also engaged in several other actions during the war which ended in February, 1674.

1689 — In 1689 King William III. incorporated "*the Admiral's Regiment*" (which was then considered the third regiment of Infantry) in the Second, now the Coldstream, regiment of Foot Guards. Two Marine regiments were, about the same time, established for service on board the fleet, which were disbanded in 1698.

1702 — On the recommencement of hostilities, in 1702, with France and Spain, both of which nations possessed powerful fleets as well as numerous armies, the British Parliament felt the expediency of enabling the Queen to increase the efficiency of her navy, by forming *Corps of Marines*, which could act at sea as well as on land.

Six regiments were accordingly added in the year 1702 to the regular Army as *Marine corps*, and six other of the regular regiments of Infantry were appointed for *Sea-service;* as shown in the following list.

The six Regiments of Marines were:—
    Colonel Thomas Saunderson's, now thirtieth foot.
    Colonel George Villiers's, now thirty-first foot.
    Colonel Edward Fox's, now thirty-second foot.
    Colonel Harry Mordaunt's; disbanded in 1713.
    Colonel Henry Holl's; disbanded in 1713.
    Colonel Viscount Shannon's; disbanded in 1713.

The six regiments of Foot for *Sea-service* were:— 1702
    Colonel Ventris Columbine's, now sixth foot.
    Colonel Thomas Erle's, now nineteenth foot.
    Colonel Gustavus Hamilton's, now twentieth foot.
    Colonel Lord Lucas's, now thirty-fourth foot.
    Colonel Earl of Donegal's, now thirty-fifth foot.
    Colonel Lord Charlemont's, now thirty-sixth foot.

Her Majesty's Order for levying this body of men was contained in the following Royal Warrant, dated 1st of June, 1702:—

" ANNE R.

    " Our pleasure is, that this establishment of
" *six regiments of Marines*, and six other regiments for
" *Sea-Service*, do commence and take place from the
" respective times of raising.
    " And our further pleasure is, that the order given
" by our dearest brother the late King, deceased, and
" such orders as are, or shall be, given by us, touching
" the pay or entertainment of our said forces, or any of
" them, or any charges thereunto belonging, shall be
" duly complied with, and that no new charge be added
" to this establishment without being communicated
" to our High Treasurer, or Commissioners of our
" Treasury for the time being.
    " Given at our Court at St. James's, on the first day
" of June in the first year of our reign.
    " *By Her Majesty's Command.*

                    " GODOLPHIN."

Other regiments were also embarked, at different periods, during the war, on board the fleet to act as Marines, and the efficiency and usefulness of these corps, while so employed, were attested by the capture of several fortresses in Spain; more especially tha of Gibraltar in 1704, the taking of which was effected by the Navy and Marines.

1702 Rules and Instructions for the better government of the Marine regiments were issued by authority of Her Majesty Queen Anne, on the 1st of July, 1702, in which it was directed, "That when on shore they were
" to be quartered in the vicinity of the dock-yards, in
" order to guard them from embezzlement, or from any
" attempt that might be made on them by an enemy."

Full instructions were also given as to their pay, subsistence, and clothing, which directed, "that the
" same deductions should be made for clothing as was
" usual in the land forces. Also that one day's pay in
" every year be deducted from officers and soldiers for
" the Hospital.

" When on board ship they were to have an equal
" proportion of provisions with the seamen, without
" any deductions from their pay, the soldiers receiving
" short allowance money like the seamen."

In order to render such portions of the Marine regiments as might be on shore, useful on all occasions when their services might be required, Her Majesty directed, that it should rest with herself, or with the Lord High Admiral, the Prince George of Denmark, to dispose of them at such places nearest to the several dock-yards as might be judged most convenient; and as there might be occasion for labourers to despatch necessary public works, Her Majesty empowered the High Admiral, or the Commissioners for executing that office, to cause to be employed in the dock-yards so many of the marine soldiers as might be judged fitting, and to make them such daily allowance for their labour, besides their ordinary pay, as should seem reasonable.

The Marine forces being thus placed under the control of the Lord High Admiral, His Royal Highness was pleased in 1702, to nominate Colonel William

Seymour (of the fourth regiment of foot) to superintend 1702 the whole, with the rank of Brigadier-General, whose peculiar duties were to observe, that the men were comfortably quartered, that the officers were attentive in their respective departments, and that the marine soldiers, when embarked on board of ship, were supplied with proper sea-clothes and other suitable necessaries. When the Marines were serving afloat, they were to be under the command of the Naval Officers of the ships.

The Uniform of the Marine forces consisted of high-crowned leather-caps, covered with cloth of the same colour as the facings of the regiment, and ornamented with devices, the same as the caps worn by the grenadiers; scarlet frock-coat; buff waist-belt; black pouch carried in front, with bayonet-belt attached; buff gaiters.

During the reign of Queen Anne, certain Independent Companies of Marines were raised for the purpose of aiding in the defence of the British possessions in the West Indies.

The first important service on which the Marine corps were employed in this reign, was on board the fleet under Admiral Sir Cloudesly Shovel, then commanding in the Mediterranean, who was instructed to make every possible arrangement, by conciliation or by conquest, among the dependencies of the French and Spanish monarchies, in order to ensure a cordial reception of the Archduke Charles of Austria, in opposition to Philip, Duke of Anjou, of France, to the throne of Spain.

After some delays, the Archduke arrived at Lisbon 1704 under Admiral Sir George Rooke, on the 25th of February, 1704, in order to concert a plan of future operations with his ally the King of Portugal.

1704 Sir George Rooke, after cruising with the fleet on the coast of Portugal, returned to Lisbon, and took the Prince of Hesse-Darmstadt on board, with whom he sailed on the 20th of April to Barcelona. On the arrival of the fleet before Barcelona, the Prince of Hesse sent a letter to Don Velasco, the governor, requiring him to surrender the town, which he refused. Information, however, being received that the city would declare for Charles III. if a show of attack were made,—sixteen hundred Marines were accordingly landed at the request, and under the command, of Major-General the Prince of Hesse-Darmstadt, on the 19th of May, 1704: this force, being found to be inadequate for the purpose, was re-embarked on the following day.

The next object of attack was the Rock of *Gibraltar*, where the Prince of Hesse landed in the afternoon of the 21st of July, 1704, with 1800 British and Dutch Marines. Acting upon the decision of a council of war, His Highness proceeded to cut off all communication with the mainland, to bombard the place, and to reduce it to the obedience of Charles III., King of Spain. The governor, on being summoned, refused to surrender, alleging that all the garrison had taken an oath of allegiance to King Philip V.

Admiral Sir George Rooke having directed a strong force to proceed against the South Mole, the enemy was driven from his guns; several boats, manned and armed, were then detached under the command of Captain Whitaker, of the Navy, who soon obtained possession of the great platform: about one hundred of the besiegers, whose impetuous bravery had carried them within the effects of a mine connected with the fort, were killed or wounded by the explosion; the rest, advancing rapidly, gained a redoubt halfway between the mole and the town. The Governor, 1704 at the urgent desire of the inhabitants, was induced to capitulate, and the Prince of Hesse took possession of the garrison on the evening of Sunday the 24th of July 1704. The loss in effecting the capture of this important fortress was sixty-one killed, and two hundred and six wounded. The attack of the seamen was one of the boldest and most difficult ever made, being obliged to climb up rocks and precipices. Thus was taken, in three days, a fortress since made impregnable to all assaults.

The loss of Gibraltar disconcerted the measures of Philip V., and of his grandfather Louis XIV. Eight thousand men, under the Marquis de Villadarias, were immediately detached from the Spanish army to retake the fortress; and the French Admiral received orders to engage the British and Dutch fleets, and to co-operate in the recapture of Gibraltar. The hostile fleets engaged on the 24th of August, about eleven leagues south of Malaga, and, after each had suffered severely, they were separated in the night. The enemy retired to Toulon, and Sir George Rooke sailed to Gibraltar. Here, after having held a Council of War, it was determined to return home; and the confederate fleet sailed for England, arriving at Spithead on the 25th of September. Sir John Leake and Admiral Vanderdussen were left at Lisbon to protect the coast of Portugal, and relieve Gibraltar, if it should be besieged as was anticipated.

The Marquis de Villadarias commenced the siege of Gibraltar on the 22nd of October, and the garrison, composed of Marines, under the command of the Prince of Hesse, sustained a siege by seven thousand men. The purpose of the enemy was to have stormed from the South Mole, united with the desperate attempt of

1704 a Spanish forlorn-hope climbing the rock, and a general attack from the mainland. The fortress was maintained against very superior numbers; and the fire of the enemy's batteries having damaged the works, a body of men was landed from the fleet to assist in the defence. Brigadier Fox, and several other officers and men, having been killed on the 5th of December, 1704, aid was solicited from the army in Portugal. Admiral Sir John Leake accordingly sailed from Lisbon on the 10th of December, with a fleet, having on board a battalion of the first and second foot guards; Barrymore's regiment, now thirteenth foot; Donegal's regiment, now thirty-fifth foot; the Dutch regiment of Waes; and a Portuguese regiment; amounting in all to upwards of three thousand men. On their passage they fell in with the enemy's squadron under Monsieur de Pointi, but they succeeded in arriving at Gibraltar, although some of the transports had separated.

These corps were safely landed on the 18th of December, and the Prince, strengthened by this reinforcement, made a sortie on the 23rd, and destroyed the lines, that had been erected within a hundred and and sixty paces of the palisade.

1705 The Marquis de Villadarias, having received a considerable reinforcement, evinced a disposition to storm the place, and on the 2nd of February, 1705, an attempt was made against the Round Tower, to ascertain what might be effected by a larger force. On the 7th the enemy attacked with five hundred chosen grenadiers, French and Walloons, commanded by Lieut.-General Thouy, and supported by one thousand Spanish troops. They ascended the hill in perfect silence at daybreak, and again attempted to storm the Round Tower, which was defended by Colonel Borr,

of the Marines, now thirty-second regiment. The as- 1705
sailants, by throwing from above great stones and grenades on his men, at last obliged him to retire into that part of the works where the foot guards were posted. Flushed with success, they advanced too far; when they were gallantly charged by Colonel Moncall, of Barrymore's (thirteenth) regiment, and driven from the Round Tower. Colonel Rivett, of the Coldstream foot-guards, having got up the rock on the right of the covered-way with twenty grenadiers, favoured very much Colonel Moncall's success. The garrison by this time had assembled, and kept up so destructive a fire that the enemy was obliged to make a precipitate retreat, losing seventy men killed on the spot; upwards of two hundred wounded; and one captain, four lieutenants, and forty men taken. The loss on the part of the garrison was twenty-seven men killed, and one hundred and twenty wounded.

Marshal de Tessé arrived with additional troops to carry on the siege; the garrison also received fresh reinforcements from Portugal, besides supplies of every description. Admiral Sir John Leake sailed from the Tagus on the 6th of March, 1705, and his arrival in the bay of Gibraltar on the 10th, was again so sudden, that he completely surprised the Baron de Pointi, together with the whole of his squadron, consisting of five ships of the line, three of which were captured, and two were driven on shore, and burnt by the enemy.

After a siege of seven months the enemy retired, in April, giving up all hopes of being able to make any impression on the fortress: his efforts were then confined to a very feeble blockade.

The fortress of Gibraltar, seated upon the territory of Spain, was thus rendered subject to the British

1705 crown by the bravery of its Navy and Marines: its possession was subsequently secured by the defence made against the renewed efforts of the Spaniards in 1727, and by the glorious defence sustained by the troops, under General Lord Heathfield, for three years, from 1779 to 1782, when it exhibited to the nations of Europe a brilliant instance of the combined exertions of the British navy and army against the repeated, but unsuccessful, attempts of Spain and France to recover this important fortress.

After the Spaniards and French had desisted from further attempts to retake Gibraltar, the Marine corps were distributed in the several ships of war which were collected in the Tagus, in order to co-operate with the land forces on the coast of Spain.

Towards the end of May, the English fleet, with about five thousand land forces on board, under the joint command of Admiral Sir Cloudesly Shovel and General the Earl of Peterborough, sailed from St. Helen's, and arrived at Lisbon on the 20th of June. King Charles went on board the Ranelagh on the 23rd of July, and the Dutch fleet having joined in the Tagus, the confederate squadron sailed on the 28th, and anchored at Gibraltar on the 11th of August. The Prince of Hesse Darmstadt, with the battalion of foot-guards, and the thirteenth and thirty-fifth regiments, embarked, and the fleet sailed for Altea Bay: form thence it again proceeded on its voyage, and anchored before Barcelona on the 22nd of August.

The Earl of Peterborough commenced active operations against *Barcelona* by an attack on the strong fortress of *Montjuich*, situated on the opposite part of the town, at which the disembarkation took place, the troops having landed near the river Bassoz, about three miles east of Barcelona, on the 23rd and 24th of 1705 August. On the 28th, King Charles went on shore, when the inhabitants of the neighbouring towns and villages flocked to the camp, and many took arms to act as guerilla-bands and miquelets. A difference of opinion on the part of the Dutch General occasioned some delay, but it was ultimately determined to attack the fortress of *Montjuich* by storm.

The storming party, consisting of four hundred grenadiers, with a support of six hundred musketeers, commanded by the Earl of Peterborough and the Prince of Hesse Darmstadt, commenced their march about ten o'clock on the night of Sunday the 13th of September round the mountains, and were followed by another detachment, and a party of dragoons. After traversing many miles of rugged mountain scenery, by different tracks, the storming party appeared about break of day at the foot of the mountain. Colonel Southwell of the sixth foot, which was then acting as Marines, was ordered to head the attack, and he succeeded in driving the enemy from the outworks into the castle. Upon this success the Prince of Hesse, advancing with great eagerness through all the fire, was shot with a musket-ball in the thigh, and upon being carried to an adjacent cottage, expired: this accident somewhat damped the spirits of the soldiers;— at the same time a large reinforcement was seen advancing from the town to aid the garrison in the Castle, and the troops received orders from some inferior officer to retire. The Earl of Peterborough rushed to the spot, countermanded the order, seized the half-pike out of Lord Charlemont's hand, and rallied and led back the soldiers to the posts they had so nobly won. The Spaniards, who were advancing

1705 from the town, turned back, and the outworks of the Fortress of Montjuich were thus gained; batteries were constructed, and the inner works were assailed with cannon-balls, bombs, and grenades. On the 17th of September the Fort surrendered, and thus facilitated the siege of the *City of Barcelona*, which was prosecuted with vigour. The Admirals even relinquished for a time their natural element, and acted on shore as General Officers;—they came daily from their ships with a body of men formed into companies, having captains and lieutenants of their own. Cannon and mortars were dragged up steep precipices by the men; and a breach being declared practicable, a body of soldiers prepared to attack the town: further effusion of blood was spared, however, by the surrender of the garrison, which capitulated on the 9th of October.

The capture of Barcelona gave additional reputation to the arms of the allies, and this splendid achievement was regarded with astonishment throughout Europe. It was accompanied by the submission of nearly all Catalonia; and Boyer, in his history of these wars, observes, "all the generals, admirals, officers, private " soldiers, and seamen, engaged in this memorable ex- " pedition, deserved each their share of the honour."

1706 King Charles and his counsellors, instead of exerting themselves to provide for the security of the towns which had come into their possession, and collecting the means for future conquests, spent their time and money in balls and public diversions. The breaches in *Barcelona*, and the fortress of *Montjuich*, were left unrepaired, and the garrison unprovided for a siege. Meanwhile King Philip was obtaining reinforcements from the favourers of his cause in Portugal, Italy, Provence, Flanders, and the Rhine, and he soon appeared at the head of above twenty thousand men to 1706 recapture the provinces he had lost. A powerful French and Spanish force approached Barcelona by land; a French fleet appeared before the town, and the garrison, being weak in numbers, regiments were hurried from other places, one English regiment travelling one hundred and twenty miles on mules, in two days, to take part in the defence of Barcelona. The siege was commenced in the beginning of April, 1706, when the soldiers repaired the breaches, and entered upon a resolute and desperate defence. A severe conflict took place on the 21st of April at *Montjuich*, in which Lord Donegal, of the thirty-fifth regiment, lost his life, and several prisoners were taken by the enemy; but when the garrison was nearly exhausted, its numbers decreased by deaths, wounds, sickness, and other causes, to about a thousand effective men, and a practicable breach was ready for the enemy to attack the place by storm, the English and Dutch fleet arrived with five regiments of foot; the French fleet hurried from before the town; and the reinforcements were landed.

The French, who had prepared to storm the place on the 10th of May, relaxed in their efforts, and raised the siege on the following day, making a precipitate retreat.

The important city of *Barcelona* being thus relieved, the fleet sailed on the 12th of May, and landed the forces of every description on the coast of Valencia. This was preparatory to an attack on *Alicant*. The capture of *Carthagena* was in the interim effected, and a garrison of six hundred marines under Major Hedges was established for its defence.

The fleet arrived off *Alicant* on the 26th of June, when the Governor-General Mahoni, was summoned to

14 FORMATION AND SERVICES OF MARINE CORPS.

1706 surrender: a refusal being made by the garrison, consisting of one thousand soldiers, and many inhabitants of the town who had volunteered in its defence, the bombardment of the city was resolved upon.

Brigadier Richard Gorges, who succeeded the Earl of Donegal, as colonel of the thirty-fifth regiment, then serving as marines, moved from Elcho on the 21st of July to within a mile of Alicant, and all the marines of the fleet, with eight hundred seamen, were landed on that day, and on the following morning:—the bombardment commenced on the evening of the 22nd. A detachment of the navy, under Admiral Sir George Byng, rendered very essential service by dismounting many of the enemy's guns on the coast. On the 24th of July the marines arrived from Carthagena, and were immediately landed; after four days the troops had gained possession of the suburbs, and all the boats were manned, and armed, in order to attack the town. On the 29th of July the ships having made a practicable breach on the Round Tower, at the west end of the place, and another at the middle of the curtain, the soldiers advanced to storm them. General Mahoni retired into the Castle, and was again summoned by Brigadier Gorges, and was at length obliged to surrender his charge on the 25th of August, after a most gallant resistance, and a heavy loss.

The fleet proceeded to *Iviça*, where it arrived on the 9th of September: the governor immediately saluted, and tendered submission to King Charles III. It was next resolved to attack *Majorca*, which surrendered on the 14th of September: a garrison of one captain, one lieutenant, and one hundred marines, was placed in this island.

1707 In June, 1707, an opportunity offered of co-operating

FORMATION AND SERVICES OF MARINE CORPS. 15

with the Duke of Savoy and Prince Eugene, in an 1707
intended attack upon Toulon: the fleet proceeded for
the coast of Italy, where it anchored, on the 28th of June,
between Nice and Antibes, about a league from the
Var: after a conference between the commanders-in-
chief, it was decided that a joint attack should be made
upon a part of the enemy's army then entrenched upon
that river: the positions, being evacuated by the enemy,
were immediately occupied by six hundred British seamen and marines: the passage was thus secured for
the Duke of Savoy to prosecute his designs, and frigates
were stationed along different parts of the sea-coast:
every aid was afforded by the fleet both as to men and
cannon; but the enemy having daily augmented his
forces, and having made a successful sally, the siege
was raised on the 10th of August, 1707, after a loss of
more than a thousand men. The French, from a sudden dread of consequences, sunk a number of their
largest ships of war, which were ever after unfit for
service.

King Charles having urged the reduction of Sardi- 1708
nia, with a view to open a passage for his troops in
Naples to attack Sicily, as well as to secure a supply of
provisions for his armies, a body of marines was withdrawn from *Tarragona,* a strong sea-port and garrison
in Catalonia, to assist in this enterprise. On the 12th
of August, 1708, the whole arrived before Cagliari, the
capital of Sardinia; and on receiving an equivocal answer
to the summons to surrender, the bombardment commenced on that evening, and continued, without inter-
mission, until the next morning, when at the break of
day Major-General Wills (thirtieth regiment) and the
whole of the marines, with one Spanish regiment, were
landed. The place, in consequence, almost immediately
surrendered.

1708 The whole having been re-embarked, the fleet again set sail on the 18th of August, 1708, for *Minorca,* and arrived at Port Mahon on the 28th of that month.

At this period *two* of the Marine regiments were drafted, and the officers and men were incorporated into the other *four,* now employed on this service: this measure had become necessary in order to supply the casualties which had occurred, and to render these corps effective. For this purpose all the marines capable of duty, were drawn from the fleet about to return home, in order to assist in the reduction of an island, which, it was expected, would make a spirited and tedious defence.

The first attack was against *Fort Fornede,* which was cannonaded by two of the ships, and surrendered after a contest of four hours; a detachment having been pushed to *Citadella* the capital, it surrendered without resistance:—the batteries were opened on the works defending the town of *Port Mahon* on the 17th of September, when, after a short but brisk fire, and the loss of only six men, a lodgment was effected under the walls of St. Philip's Castle; and on the next day the place surrendered.

Thus was this strong fortress, and the important *Island of Minorca,* gained by a force of only two thousand four hundred men; the garrison consisted of one thousand soldiers, with upwards of one hundred pieces of cannon mounted.

Admiral Sir George Byng arrived at Lisbon on the 14th of October, from Portsmouth, having Her Majesty the Queen of Portugal on board; but although many other objects of service were in contemplation, nothing further was attempted during the remainder of the year 1708.

On the 28th of October, 1708, the decease of His Royal

Highness the Prince George of Denmark, Consort of 1708
Her Majesty Queen Anne, and Lord High Admiral of
England, took place.

In the early part of the year 1709 a plan was formed 1709
to attack *Port Royal* in the province of Nova Scotia,
at that time in possession of the French: for this
purpose a body of four hundred marines was embarked,
and the expedition was entrusted to the joint conduct
of Colonel Nicholson of the Marine forces, and Captain
Martin of the Navy. The squadron proceeded for
Boston, where they were reinforced by some ships,
and provincial auxiliaries: for this intended conquest
a council of war was held, and arrangements were
made for the debarkation of a body consisting of two
thousand five hundred men, which took place on the
24th of September. On the 1st of October the Governor surrendered the fortress, and a garrison of
Marines took possession. The fortress was named
Anna-polis Royal, in honour of Queen Anne, in whose
reign it was conquered.

At this period the prospects of King Charles III. in
obtaining the monarchy of Spain, had become very
gloomy and doubtful. The town of Alicant had sustained a long and obstinate siege, against very powerful
forces of Spain and France. The garrison, consisting
principally of Marines, exhibited the most heroic perseverance in maintaining the place. The fleet under
Admiral Sir George Byng, and the troops on board,
under the command of General Stanhope, were to
have attempted its relief, and the squadron was at the
same time to have attacked the enemy's lines along
the sea-shore; but the weather continuing severe, and
heavy gales preventing communication with the town,
the Commander-in-Chief deemed it necessary to

1709 propose terms of surrender, and the remainder of the brave troops were embarked on board of the fleet, which now proceeded to Tarragona, Port Mahon, and afterwards to Barcelona. During the remainder of the year 1709, the fleets attempted nothing beyond the protecting of the convoys of provisions, where they were considered necessary, and in harassing the commerce of the enemy.

1710   On the 13th of March, 1710, Admiral Sir John Norris arrived at Port Mahon, as Commander-in-Chief of the Naval forces. After making arrangements for disposing of the ships and troops in attacks upon the enemy, he proceeded to Barcelona on the 18th of June, in order to concert future operations with His Majesty King Charles III.

An expedition was planned against the *Isle of Cette* in the province of Languedoc, where the troops and Marines were landed on the 13th of July. The place made a feeble resistance, and the Fort, upon which were mounted eighteen pieces of cannon, surrendered on the same day. The regiment of Stanhope, and three hundred Marines, advanced against Adge, and the town was delivered up without resistance.

The Isle of Cette was shortly afterwards recovered by the French army, under the Duke of Roquetaine; but the British troops had previously re-embarked.

1711   In the early part of the year 1711 it was resolved to make an attack on the town of *Quebec*, the capital of the French possessions in Canada, for which service Admiral Sir Hovenden Walker and Major-General John Hill were appointed Commanders-in-Chief: a large fleet of ships of war formed part of the armament, which was to be further strengthened by troops from the American colonies; they were directed to proceed to Boston in New England, and to make arrangements for this undertaking. They reached Naerlaskel near Boston on the 24th of June, and having collected the provincial corps, and withdrawn the Marines from Anna-polis Royal, which had been occupied by these corps since its surrender in 1709, they sailed for the object of their destination, after many delays, on the 30th of July.

The expedition did not reach the River St. Lawrence until the 21st of August, when it encountered storms, and being furnished with pilots who were unacquainted with the navigation of that river, eight transports, a store ship, and a sloop were lost by shipwreck, and upwards of eighty persons, including officers, soldiers, and women, principally belonging to Colonel Kane's fourth regiment, and Colonel Clayton's thirty-seventh regiment, perished in this fatal service.

A scarcity of provisions had arisen, and it was then determined by a council of war that further operations should be abandoned. Some of the corps proceeded to Anna-polis Royal, and the squadron returned to England in the month of October, 1711, after having left the provincial auxiliaries upon their own coast.

On the 17th of April, 1711, the decease of Joseph I., Emperor of Germany, occurred, and Charles III., of Spain, was elected Emperor of Germany at Frankfort, by the name of Charles IV., on the 12th October following. Further attempts on the part of the British Government, in the cause of King Charles were now unnecessary, as he was called upon to assume the Imperial throne of his country. His Majesty embarked at Barcelona, on the 27th of September, on board of the confederate fleet, and sailed for Italy.

In the year 1712 negotiations were entered into by

1713 Great Britain and France, and peace was restored by the treaty of Utrecht on the 31st of March, 1713. By this treaty it was settled, that Great Britain should retain possession of Gibraltar, Minorca, and Nova Scotia, which had been conquered during the late war, and in effecting which, the Marine corps, which had been formed during the reign of Queen Anne, greatly contributed.

1714 On the return of peace, as concluded by the treaty of Utrecht, in 1713, the corps of Marines, which had been formed in the reign of Queen Anne, were ordered to be disbanded; they were considered to be part of a war establishment, and a spirit of public economy, as well as of jealousy against a standing army, particularly in the early periods after the Revolution of 1688, afforded to the leaders of parliamentary debates, and of popular prejudices, grounds of objection to the maintaining of such corps after the termination of hostilities.

The arrangements consequent on the general peace having been made, a great reduction in the forces took place. These arrangements had scarcely been decided, when the decease of Her Majesty Queen Anne took place on the 1st of August, 1714, and King George the First ascended the throne.

Soon after His Majesty's accession, the peace of the kingdom was disturbed by the hostile designs of King Louis XV. of France, who had supported and encouraged James Francis Edward Stuart, son of His late Majesty King James II., in his endeavours to obtain the throne of Great Britain; but the loyalty of the people, and the courage of the troops, defeated the attempts for the restoration of the Stuart family.

King George I., being supported by the parliament,

adopted active measures for increasing his army, and resisting the plans of his enemies. Six additional regiments of cavalry, from ninth to fourteenth dragoons, were raised. The establishments of the regiments of infantry were increased, and in consideration of the gallant and extensive services of the Marine corps during the late war, Wills's, now *thirtieth,* Goring's, now *thirty-first,* and Borr's, now *thirty-second,* were incorporated with the regiments of infantry of the line, and ranked according to the dates of their original formation in 1702.

From the year 1714 to 1739 no corps of Marines, except four invalid companies, were kept on the establishment of the army.

For several years Spain had beheld with great jealousy the growing commerce and increasing naval consequence of Great Britain, particularly in the neighbourhood of her possessions in South America, where Spain had endeavoured to monopolize the whole commerce and wealth of Mexico and Peru; the vessels of foreign powers were forbidden, under severe penalties, to approach within a certain distance of her American possessions; and to enforce this, the American seas were filled with Spanish cruisers, whose enormities at length attracted the attention of the British parliament. After fruitless representations to the court of Madrid for redress, the British ministry at length determined on hostilities; and, with the acclamations of the nation, war was formally declared against Spain on the 23rd of October, 1739.

It was again considered necessary to form an efficient maritime force in distinct regiments, by which means the corps of the regular army could be embarked when required for continental services, and the marine regi-

1739 ments could be employed, either on board of ships of war, or at the naval stations, as might be considered best for the public service.

Orders were issued for augmenting the land-forces, and also for forming *six regiments of marines*, each to consist of ten companies of seventy privates in each company, and to be commanded by

    1st, Colonel Edward Wolfe, from 3rd Foot Guards;
    2nd, Colonel W. Robinson, from Handasyd's 22nd regiment;
    3rd, Colonel Andrew Lowther, from 2nd Foot Guards;
    4th, Colonel John Wynyard, from Tyrrell's regiment;
    5th, Colonel Charles Douglas, from Howard's regiment;
    6th, Colonel Lucius Ducie Moreton, from 3rd Foot Guards.

In order to facilitate the speedy formation of these corps, and to render them effective, five men from each company of the regiments of foot-guards were appointed serjeants and corporals; and further, that they might be rapidly completed, a bounty of thirty shillings per man was allowed to 1800 men who volunteered from the regiments of infantry to the marine corps: by these energies, the whole of the marine regiments were soon raised and disciplined.

On the prospect of the commencement of hostilities Admiral Vernon had sailed for Jamaica, where he arrived in October, 1739, with a fleet of five ships, having 200 marines on board, and proceeded from thence to *Porto Bello*, the destined object of his attack, which was at that time the great mart for the wealthy commerce of Chili and Peru; the attempt was fraught with many difficulties, but it was undertaken and performed with spirit and promptitude.

On the 21st of November, 1739, the attack was commenced by the ships, in line of battle, against the Iron Castle, a strong fort at the north point of the entrance into the harbour. The Spaniards flying from several parts of it, an instant debarkation of the seamen and marines from on board the Burford, Norwich, and Worcester took place under cover of those ships, and the fort was carried. Upon the 22nd an attack was intended against the whole, but the enemy displayed the white flag as a signal of surrender. After destroying the fortifications, which from their strength required some time, the Admiral with his squadron sailed for Jamaica on the 13th of December, 1739.

1739

In the year 1740 an additional regiment, of four battalions, was authorised to be raised in America, and the royal standard was erected at New York, as the signal-post to which every volunteer marine was to repair. The field officers and subalterns were appointed by the King, and the captains of companies were nominated by the American provinces. Colonel Spotswood, of Virginia, was appointed colonel-commandant of the whole. It was supposed that, from climate, the natives of that continent were better calculated for the service to which they were destined, than Europeans. Their uniform was camblet coats, brown linen waistcoats, and canvas trousers. This regiment, which was afterwards commanded by Colonel Gooche, was considered as the FORTY-THIRD regiment of infantry of the line.

1740

In January, 1740, an augmentation of 340 men, and of one lieutenant in each company, was made in each of the six regiments of marines, and twenty men were added to each of the four companies of invalids, and a similar number to the retired marine establishment.

The utility of the corps of marines was now universally admitted, and in a letter addressed to the Duke of Newcastle, then first lord of the treasury and prime

1740 minister, by Admiral Vernon, previously to his sailing with an expedition to the West Indies, he thus expressed himself on the subject of marine soldiers:—

"I could wish that we" (alluding to ships of war) "had each a company of regular troops on board, "which would strengthen us in numbers, and their "expertness in handling their arms would incite our "seamen to the imitation of them. If we should come "to a general war with France as well as Spain, I be- "lieve your Grace will have already perceived, from "the difficulty of manning our ships, the necessity of "converting most of our marching regiments into "marines.

"I have always looked upon our fleet as what must "not only protect our trade, but secure to us the "blessings of a Protestant succession, being strongly "convinced in my own judgment, that preserving a "superiority at sea is the best security of His Majes- "ty's government, as well as the trade and prosperity "of this kingdom."

The sentiments expressed by Admiral Vernon, in favour of the marines, were drawn from the acknowledged usefulness of the corps so employed in the naval expeditions during the reign of Queen Anne.

In the year 1740 *four* additional regiments of marines were raised, viz.:—

7th, Colonel W. Cornwall; 9th, Colonel C. Powlett;
8th, Colonel W. Hanmore; 10th, Colonel J. Jeffreys.

Each regiment consisted of ten companies of 100 men in each company, which, with officers included, amounted to 1155 in each regiment. The *six* regiments raised in 1739 were increased to the same numbers of officers and men.

In February, 1740, the town of *Carthagena*, the 1740 capital of an extensive and wealthy province in Terra Firma in South America, was bombarded, and an attack was made upon Chagre, a fort situate upon the mouth of a river of that name a little to the northwest of the Gulf of Darien. The latter surrendered, after a sharp contest, on the 24th of March, when the castle, situated on a rock, and the custom-house under its protection, were demolished and burnt.

These were all that could be performed until the arrival of reinforcements and supplies from England. The fleet afterwards returned to Porto Bello, and from thence to Jamaica.

Considerable exertions were made in England during the year 1740 with the view of attacking, more effectually, the Spanish possessions in South America.

A large number of ships of war was assembled at Spithead under the command of Rear-Admiral Sir Chaloner Ogle, and a land-force, consisting of Harrison's (15th) regiment, Wentworth's (24th) regiment, and part of Cavendish's (34th) regiment, was collected in the Isle of Wight, and held in readiness, with the six regiments of marines, to be embarked for service under the orders of General Lord Cathcart, a nobleman of approved courage and experience in war.

The fleet, with the British armament, consisting of one hundred and seventy ships, sailed from St. Helen's in October, 1740; but being overtaken by a tempest in the Bay of Biscay, it was dispersed. The greater part of the vessels, being re-collected, the Admiral prosecuted his voyage, and anchored at the neutral island of Dominica, in order to obtain a supply of wood and water.

Unfortunately for the service, General Lord Cath-

1740 cart fell an early victim to the disease of the climate, and the command of the expedition devolved upon Brigadier-General Thomas Wentworth, of the 24th regiment.

The sixth regiment of foot, under the command of Colonel John Guise, who was appointed brigadier-general, was subsequently ordered to proceed to the West Indies to reinforce the troops employed in this enterprise.

1741 The fleet, under the charge of Rear-Admiral Sir Chaloner Ogle, arrived at Jamaica in January, 1741, and joined the force under Vice-Admiral Vernon, who was thus placed at the head of the most formidable fleet and army which were ever employed in those seas. The conjoined squadrons consisted of twenty-nine ships of the line, with nearly an equal number of frigates, fire-ships, and bomb-ketches, well manned, and plentifully supplied with provisions, stores, and necessaries. The number of seamen amounted to 15,000; that of the land-forces, including the American regiment of four battalions (Colonel Spotswood's) and a body of negroes enlisted at Jamaica, did not fall short of 12,000.

The whole force sailed from Irish Bay in Hispaniola, and anchored on the evening of the 4th of March in the *Grande Playa*, to windward of the town of *Carthagena*, the intended object of the attack.

The necessary arrangements having been made, the fleet moved forward in two divisions on the 8th of March, in order to silence the different forts, preparatory to the landing of the troops.

After about one hour's cannonade, the forts of *St. Jago* and *St. Philip* were deserted by the enemy, and were taken possession of by the troops; and by the 15th all the soldiers, with their tents, tools, artillery, and stores, were landed, the ground cleared, and an encampment 1741 formed.

The reduction of the Castle of *Bocca Chica* next took place, which, on a practicable breach being made, it was determined to storm; but, in consequence of a well-judged diversion of the navy, the Spaniards retired without firing a shot, and when the grenadiers advanced to storm at the hour appointed, they met no resistance.

A panic had seized the enemy, who set fire to one of their ships; taking advantage of this state, the boats resolved to attempt the fort of *St. Joseph*, which was immediately evacuated. The Spaniards appearing to be determined to sink their vessels, the British crews proceeded to board the ship Galicia, which carried the flag of the Spanish Admiral.

After various services the castle of *Grande Castello* was gained, and the enemy had sunk all their ships of war; preparations were made for landing the troops near the town, in order to cut off all communication with the main land.

Two channels having been made through the sunk vessels, with which the Spaniards had blocked up the entrance of the harbour, the troops and artillery were re-embarked, and commenced landing on the 5th of April near the city; and, after a spirited contest, the British bivouacked within a mile of the castle of *St. Lazar*, which commanded the town. The men passed three nights in the open air for want of tents and tools, which could not be landed sooner, and the health of the troops became seriously injured.

As affairs were now drawing to extremities, and the men were fast diminishing in numbers from hard duty and the effects of climate, Brigadier-General Wentworth resolved to attack *St. Lazar* by escalade, it

1741 being judged necessary to forego the ceremonies of a regular siege, and, however hazardous, to rest the issue upon a storm.

Accordingly before daybreak on the 9th of April, a force under the command of Brigadier-General Guise, of the sixth foot, consisting of five hundred grenadiers, supported by a thousand Marines, and some American and Jamaican levies, advanced against the enemy's lines in front of the fort; these were followed by a body of Americans, with woolpacks, scaling-ladders and hand-grenades.

The grenadiers, led by Colonel Grant, of the fifth Marines, rushed forward with astonishing bravery, and, leaping into the entrenchments, carried the works in gallant style, driving the Spaniards into the fort over a drawbridge which communicated with the lines. Colonel Grant fell mortally wounded, and the troops, after sustaining a most destructive fire for several hours with intrepidity and perseverance, were ordered to retreat, having lost many officers, and 600 men in killed and wounded.

This repulse was succeeded by the violent periodical rains; the country was deluged with water; and the change of atmosphere, which is always attended with epidemical diseases, produced the most fatal effects. The troops were so drenched with rain, and their health so seriously impaired, that all hope of further success vanished; they were accordingly re-embarked, and the forts and castle of the harbour of *Carthagena* having been demolished, the fleet sailed for Jamaica on the 6th of May, where it arrived on the 9th of that month. After re-embarking, the distempers, peculiar to the climate, produced numerous casualties among the troops.

Thus terminated, for the time, the expedition to

Spanish South America, during which the persevering 1741 and undaunted bravery of British Seamen, Soldiers, and Marines, and their patient endurance under the most trying difficulties, were never displayed in a greater degree.

In consequence of the heavy losses sustained at *Carthagena*, and the mortality which continued to prevail after the troops returned to Jamaica, it was not until the beginning of July, 1741, that the fleet and army were in a condition to renew their operations. It was then resolved to proceed against the *Island of Cuba*, where they anchored on the 18th of July in Waltenham Bay, about eighteen leagues to windward of *St. Jago*, the first object of their intended attack. The troops were landed on the 24th, consisting of nearly 4,000 men, including 1000, negroes raised by the Island of Jamaica, with a view to sustain the peculiar duties of fatigue, naturally expected to arise on this service.

After establishing a position on the side of the river, nearly three leagues from the mouth of the harbour, the General pushed some detachments into the country, which beat back the outposts of the enemy, and in a few days returned to the camp with plentiful supplies of provisions.

It was originally intended by the Commanders-in-Chief to have made a joint attack upon *St. Jago*, but the want of unanimity ruined every purpose, and contentious debates and dilatory measures, instead of cordial co-operation and daring enterprise, took place; while the interests of the country, and the lives of the troops, were sacrificed to the prejudices and bad judgment of the officers entrusted with so important a command.

After an interval of several months, during which

1741 nothing was attempted towards effecting the conquest of the island, and when sickness, the never-failing result of inactivity, particularly in those climes, began its ravages, it was determined to evacuate the island, which took place on the 20th of November, 1741, when the regimental Returns were as follow :—

Regiment.		Colonels.	Serjeants, Drummers, and Rank and File.
15th regiment		Harrison . . .	225
24th regiment		Wentworth . .	219
43rd regiment ⎧ 1st Battalion		Spotswood's, afterwards Gooche's, Marines	159
American ⎨ 2nd ,,			110
Marines ⎩ 3rd ,,			99
4th ,,			121
1st Marines (aft^ds. 44th Rt.)		Wolfe	181
2nd do. . (,, 45th Rt.)		Fraser	158
3rd do. . (,, 46th Rt.)		Lowther . . .	237
4th do. . (,, 47th Rt.)		Wynyard . . .	177
5th do. . (,, 48th Rt.)		Cochrane . . .	191
6th do. . (,, 49th Rt.)		Cotterell . . .	211
			2088
Sick in all			566
Total			2654

The total loss of officers at the close of 1741 amounted to one Commander-in-Chief, five colonels, ten lieut.-colonels, seven majors, fifty-five captains, one hundred and sixteen subalterns, and fourteen staff officers.

The heavy casualties in the Marine regiments are shown when it is stated that these six regiments consisted of more than one thousand men each, and that only 2654 men returned.

The foregoing statement affords a sad record of the ill-judged plans relating to the expedition to South America, both as to the season of the year at which it was undertaken, and the deficiency of means and arrangements with which it was attempted to be carried into execution. Great disappointment and dissatisfaction were consequently created in the feelings of the British public.

The transports returned to Jamaica on the 29th of November, 1741, and the squadron continued at sea to meet the reinforcements which were anxiously expected from England.

In January 1742, nearly 3000 men, including 2000 Marines, arrived at Jamaica. Another expedition was now meditated, which put to sea early in March; but adverse winds, the separation of the transports having on board the working negroes, and the expectation of the periodical rains being then about to set in, suggested to a Council of War, held at Porto Bello, at the close of that month, the immediate return of the whole armament to the port they had left: the fleet arrived at Jamaica upon the 15th of May.

It was now considered desirable to detach a force to take possession of *Rattan*, an island in the Bay of Honduras, and a situation proper for maintaining a commercial intercourse with South America, as well as the trade in logwood. An establishment having been formed there in the early part of the year, it was determined in a Council of War to send a force of 50 marines and 200 Americans, under Major Caulfield, in order to place the island in a state of military defence.

On the 23rd of August the troops reached *Port Royal*, on the south side of the island, where they formed a camp and erected *Fort George* to defend the harbour, as well as *Fort Frederick* on the western part of it. A proportion of the Americans, who were papists, formed a plot to render the settlement abortive, and to rise upon the Marines. Her Majesty's ship, the Litchfield, then in the harbour, hearing the alarm-guns, instantly landed her party of Marines, who,

1742 with those on shore, soon checked the daring mutiny, secured the delinquents, and preserved the settlement to the British Crown.

At this period it was necessary to detach 500 men to the assistance of *General Oglethorpe*, in *South Carolina*, and to repel the menaces of the Spaniards against the infant colony of *Georgia*.*

On the 23rd of September orders arrived at Jamaica for the recal of Admiral Vernon and of General Wentworth; for providing the fleet with a number of men from the Marines, sufficient to supply its wants; and also to fill up the vacancies in the eight Independent Companies raised for the defence of Jamaica (now the 49th Regiment):—These services absorbed all the men who were considered fit for duty, and the remainder were embarked for England.

After the departure of Admiral Vernon, the Naval Command devolved on Sir Chaloner Ogle, who bore his testimony to the zeal and bravery of the troops, whose gallant efforts and patient endurance, under great privations, had been conspicuous throughout a series of misfortunes. Upwards of 7000 Marines and nearly 4000 other troops were the lamentable victims to pestilence and disease, but not to defeat; and the objects which had been effected, although not adequate to the hopes and expectations of the British Nation,

---

* In 1732 trustees were appointed by charter to superintend a new settlement in *Georgia*, situated to the southward of *Carolina* in America, and *Mr. James Oglethorpe*, General and Governor of the Province, embarked at Gravesend with a number of poor families to plant that Colony. In 1737, when the King of Spain claimed as part of his territories, the Colony of Georgia, which was considered to belong to Great Britain, General Oglethorpe was authorised to raise a regiment of six companies of 100 men each, for the defence of the settlement. The colonies of Georgia and Carolina had been named from King George II., and his consort Queen Caroline.

FORMATION AND SERVICES OF MARINE CORPS. 33

were distressing to the enemy, and embarrassing to the Spanish Government. 1742

In the early part of 1743 it was resolved to make another attempt upon the continent of South America, and the conduct of the operations was entrusted to Captain Knowles, of the Navy, who had on board of his squadron 400 of *Dalzell's* (thirty-eighth) *regiment* and about *six hundred Marines*. They were first ordered to rendezvous at Antigua, from which island they sailed on the 12th of February with a view to an attack upon La Guira, a town in the district of the Caraccas in Terra Firma. The attack was commenced on the 18th, but, owing to a heavy swell, the ships could not approach the shore, and the troops were consequently not landed. After a heavy cannonade, which was ended only by the night, the ships withdrew from the combat: the town suffered extremely, many breaches being made in the fortifications; and the enemy sustained a loss of more than 700 men. The British squadron suffered considerable damage, and had nearly 400 men killed and wounded. 1743

The fleet proceeded to Curaçoa to refit, where preparations were made for another attempt upon the sea-coast of Terra Firma. Having been reinforced by some Dutch volunteers, Commodore Knowles sailed from this island on the 20th of March, and steered for *Porto Cavallo*, a town having a respectable force, and being in a good state of defence.

On the 15th of April the ships anchored to the eastward of the town, and on the 16th two vessels commenced a flanking fire against *Ponta Brava;* and after the batteries were silenced, it was decided to land the troops in order to take possession, and to turn the guns against the castle, their retreat being secured by a

D

1743 ship of war within pistol-shot of the shore: by sunset the ships had accomplished their object, and by dusk a force of 1200 sailors, soldiers, and Dutch volunteers, was disembarked under the command of Major Lucas.

About eleven at night the van had gained one of the fascine batteries upon Ponta Brava, but the garrison having been alarmed, and being prepared for resistance, this mixed detachment acted under the influence of a panic, and retreated with precipitation to the ships. On the 21st it was resolved to make another attack of the squadron and forces against the castle and fascine batteries: four ships were destined to batter the former on the 24th, while three others were placed against the latter. The cannonading began at eleven on the noon of that day, and was maintained with mutual obstinacy till night, when, some of the ships having expended their ammunition, and others being damaged, they were ordered to anchor beyond reach of the enemy's shot. This attack being fruitless, and the troops being prevented from landing, it was deemed impracticable to push the enterprise any further: it was accordingly resolved on the 28th of April to return to Jamaica.

From the period of the commencement of hostilities against Spain in 1739, the conduct of the Court of Versailles had been equivocal, and in the beginning of the year 1743 the projects of Louis XV. were developed by the equipment of powerful naval armaments in the ports of France, and by the assembling of armies on the sea-coasts, the avowed aim of which was against the Crown and liberties of the British Empire.

Being no longer able to restrain her views, France

declared war on the 20th of March, 1743, which was 1743 answered by a proclamation on the part of Great Britain on the 31st of that month.

A force of 11,550 Marines was granted by Parlia- 1744 ment as a part of the establishment for the year 1744, at which period fleets were detached to every quarter of the globe. A partial affair occurred in the Mediterranean in May of this year, in which a party of Marines disembarked from the Essex ship of war, and signalized themselves: that ship being on a cruise gained sight of twenty-six xebeques and settees, bound to Antibes, from whence they were to carry troops to Italy: the former were a convoy to the latter, which were laden with powder, cannon, ordnance stores, and provisions: thirteen having taken refuge in the Creek of Casse, the Marines were landed in order to co-operate with the boats, and to repel any enemy that might appear to retard their progress: they were attacked by a body of Spaniards, whom they beat back, and thus effected the object on which they were employed: eleven vessels were burnt and two captured.

The most active measures were adopted, by order of the Secretary at War, for again completing the ten regiments of Marines, in order to render them effective as speedily as possible.

Attacks having been made during the last year by 1745 the French upon *Canso* and *Anna-polis* in *Nova Scotia*, the former of which they burnt, the Northern Colonies of British America became alarmed for their safety: an expedition was consequently commenced against *Louisburg;* considerable levies were raised in the American provinces, and a co-operating naval force, under Commodore Warren, then commanding on the

1745 West India station, was ordered to repair to Canso; the arrangements made for conducting this expedition were carried into effect with that confidence and secrecy which are always essential towards securing the success of a military enterprise, and the exertions of the Americans were fully equal to the important interests which they had at stake.

On the 4th of April the levies from New England, having reached *Canso*, were encamped and brought into military order and discipline preparatory to the arrival of other corps from the several provinces, while the ships of war upon the coast, and some stout privateers, continued off the harbour of *Louisburg*, in order to cut off all intelligence of the projected enterprise. On the 23rd of April Commodore Warren arrived at *Canso*, and by the 29th all the land-forces were embarked, and proceeded to *Gabaras Bay*, about four miles from the capital of *Cape Breton*.

On the 30th of April 2000 men were landed at noon, who beat back a detachment of troops which was sent to prevent their disembarkation. On that and the following day three hundred seamen and *five hundred Marines* were disembarked under cover of the vessels ranged along the coast. The troops were under the command of Brigadier-General William Pepperell, a native of Piccataway, and Colonel of American Militia.

The French, conscious of the strength of their positions, maintained possession of the city until their means of defence were overpowered by the forces brought against them.

By indefatigable labour, the British Marines, and the American provincials, succeeded in effecting an entrance into the harbour on the 1st of June, 1745; *Louisburg* capitulated, and with it the whole dependency of *Cape Breton;* the object was attained with a loss little exceeding 100 men.* 1745

Two regiments were formed for service at Cape Breton, by Colonel William Shirley and Sir William Pepperell, each consisting of ten companies of 100 men per company : these were numbered the 50th and 51st regiments of infantry of the line.

In the year 1746 very serious complaints were made of the neglect and delay which had occurred in the settlement of the accounts of the Marine Corps, and a committee was appointed to investigate the grievances which had been represented. The cause of the delay was alleged to arise, in the first instance, from the absence of regular and periodical muster-rolls, according to the practice in regiments of the regular army. This system, it was stated, could not easily be acted upon in the corps of Marines, who were employed by detachments in the several ships of war. The investigation produced, however, the effect of a large balance in the hands of the Paymaster-General being repaid into the Bank of England, for the benefit of those who were justly entitled to it. 1746

The privations and inconveniences, which this meritorious body of troops had continued to endure for several years, did not affect their loyalty and steady allegiance, and they still remained the useful corps, in periods of emergency, they had always proved in former years.

For the service of this year (1746) nearly 12,000 Marines were included in the parliamentary vote of the military establishment. An expedition against

---

* Cape Breton was restored to the French after the peace of Aix-la-Chapelle in 1748. It was retaken in 1758 by Admiral Boscawen and General Sir Jeffery Amherst, and finally ceded to Great Britain at the peace of 1763.

1746 Quebec was contemplated at this period, and a considerable force was assembled at Spithead with that intent, but delays took place until the season for such an attempt became too late. Of this force Colonel Powlett's (the ninth) regiment of Marines formed a part.

The troops were afterwards destined against *Port L'Orient*, under the directions of Admiral Lestock and Lieut.-General Sinclair. Sixteen sail of the line and eight frigates, with 5000 troops, exclusive of Marines, were the number employed on this occasion. The long detention of so respectable a force until the period of the equinox, endangered its progress along a hostile coast at so critical a season, and gave time for the enemy to ascertain the object of the expedition.

The fleet sailed from Plymouth on the 14th of September for the coast of Brittany, and a debarkation of the troops was effected on the 20th of that month, in *Quimperlay Bay*: on the 21st the troops advanced in two columns against *Plymeur*, which surrendered, and on the following day the whole moved on to a rising ground within a mile of *Port L'Orient*, the ultimate object of their views. Some affairs took place between the 21st and 26th of September, when after a cannonade, which did considerable damage to the town, a retreat was commenced under cover of the night. The French were pouring in from all quarters, and the situation of the British troops became critical.

After a loss of 150 men killed, wounded, and missing, a re-embarkation was effected, and the fleet sailed on the 1st of October for the Bay of Borneuff, off Quiberon, to the south of Quimperlay: a detachment of Marines was entrenched at Quimperlay to guard the landing-place; the remainder, under Colonel Holmes, was united with the army : some troops were landed on the 4th of October on the peninsula of 1746 Quiberon, and, after remaining ashore some days, the whole returned to England.

The number of Marines for the year 1747 was 1747 eleven thousand one hundred and fifty, as included in the parliamentary vote of that year.

On the 28th of February, 1747, His Majesty King George II. directed, that the several regiments of Marines, which were then existing, or might hereafter be raised, should be placed under the entire command of the Lords Commissioners for executing the office of High Admiral of Great Britain and Ireland.

The following Royal Warrant was issued on this subject :—

" *To Our Commissioners for executing the office of High*
 " *Admiral of Our Kingdom of Great Britain and*
 " *Ireland; and to Our Commissioners for executing*
 " *the office of our High Admiral for the time being.*"

(Copy)

" Whereas We have thought it necessary for the
" good of Our Service to put under your immediate
" and entire command all our Marine regiments now
" raised, or hereafter to be raised ; Our Will and
" Pleasure therefore is, that you do take upon you
" the immediate and entire command of the said
" Marine forces accordingly ; and for the better go-
" vernment of our said Marine regiments, we have
" thought fit to empower and authorise you to prepare
" and publish such rules and ordinances as are fit to
" be observed by our said Marine forces under your
" command, hereby strictly charging and requiring the
" several colonels and other officers, who shall from time
" to time be employed in the said regiments, to take
" notice thereof, and in all respects to conform them-
" selves to such directions accordingly, and to cause
" exact musters to be taken of them, as well at sea as
" on shore, and that the same be transmitted to our

1747 " Commissary-General of Marines, in order to the more
" speedy clearing of the accounts of our said Marine
" regiments. And whereas, by the establishment,
" provision is made for such contingent charges as may
" arise in this service, and to the use of our said forces,
" you are hereby further authorized to direct the
" payment of the said money, in such proportions as
" you shall, in your discretion, think necessary, for the
" purpose aforesaid.

" And for executing the several powers and autho-
" rities herein expressed this shall be your warrant.
" And so we bid you heartily farewell.

   " Given at our Court at St. James's, this 28th
   " February, 1746-7, in the 20th year of
   " our reign.
    " By His Majesty's Command.
    (Signed) " CHESTERFIELD."

Notwithstanding the disasters which had attended the expeditions of the French in North America in the preceding year (1746), when Louis XV. had equipped an extensive armament, under the command of the Duke d'Anville for the recapture of Cape Breton, which was rendered ineffectual by storms and other casualties, and by the death of its commander, the French Monarch was not discouraged by these disasters; but was resolved to renew his efforts against the British colonies in North America, and also the settlements in the East Indies. For these purposes two squadrons were prepared at Brest, one commanded by Commodore de la Jonquière, and the other, destined for India, by Monsieur de St. George.

Intelligence had been received by the British Government of these preparations, and measures were adopted in order to counteract the views of the enemy. The occasion afforded a renewed display of the zeal and intrepidity of Vice-Admiral Anson and Rear-

Admiral Warren, who sailed from Plymouth on the 9th of April, in order to intercept both squadrons, which were to set sail together. The Vice-Admiral, on board of the " Prince George " of ninety guns, with the Rear-Admiral, on board the " Devonshire," and twelve ships more under his command, received directions to cruize between Ushant and Cape Finisterre on the coast of Galicia.

1747

On the 3rd of May, 1747, they fell in with the French squadrons, consisting of six large ships of war, as many frigates, and four armed vessels equipped by the French East India Company, having under their convoy about thirty ships laden with merchandize: those prepared for war immediately shortened sail, and formed in line of battle, while the rest, under the protection of the six frigates, proceeded on their voyage with all the sail they could carry. The British squadron was likewise drawn up in line of battle, and the engagement began with great fury about four o'clock in the afternoon. The enemy's ships sustained the battle with equal conduct and valour, until they were overpowered by numbers, and they then struck their colours. About seven hundred of the French were killed and wounded in this action; the English lost about five hundred; and among them Captain Grenville, Commander of the ship " Defiance," nephew to Lord Viscount Cobham, an officer of the most promising genius, and animated with the noblest sentiments of honour and patriotism. Two of these prizes were the " *Invincible* " and the " *Glory*," which induced the Captain of the former to say to the Admiral, on giving up his sword, "Sir, you have conquered the *Invincible,* and *Glory* follows you." This blow was severely felt by France, who had vainly flattered herself, that by means of this armament she should

1747 render herself mistress of the Indian seas, and by that superiority be enabled to wrest from the British their most valuable possessions in that part of the world.

A considerable quantity of money, intended to answer the contingencies of these expeditions, was found on board of the French ships, which were brought to Spithead, and the treasure, being landed, was conveyed in twenty waggons to the Bank of England, escorted by a party of Marines, amidst the acclamations of the populace.

For this achievement Vice-Admiral George Anson was created a Peer of Great Britain, and Rear-Admiral Peter Warren was invested with the Order of the Bath. The whole fleet received the thanks of the Sovereign, through their Commander, Admiral Lord Anson.

The year 1747 was remarkable for other naval successes; about the middle of June, COMMODORE FOX, with six ships of war, cruizing in the latitude of Cape Ortegal, in Galicia, took about forty French ships, richly laden from St. Domingo, after they had been abandoned by their convoy.

The fourteenth of October, 1747, was rendered memorable as another day of triumph for the British Navy. REAR-ADMIRAL EDWARD HAWKE sailed from Plymouth in the beginning of August, with fourteen ships of the line, with instructions to intercept a fleet of French merchant-ships bound for the West Indies: the British fleet cruized for some time on the coast of Bretagne, and the French ships sailed from the Isle of Aix under convoy of nine ships of the line, besides frigates, commanded by M. de l'Etendiere. The two squadrons came in sight of each other in the latitude of Belle Isle. The battle commenced about eleven in the forenoon, and lasted

FORMATION AND SERVICES OF MARINE CORPS. 43

until night, when all the French squadron, except two 1747 ships, the "Intrepide" and "Tonnant," which escaped in the dark, had struck to the English flag. After despatching a sloop to Commodore Legge, commanding a squadron in the Leeward Islands, to take proper measures to intercept the French ships in the passage to Martinique, and other French islands, ADMIRAL HAWKE conducted his prizes to Spithead, and was rewarded with the Order of the Bath; and the thanks of a grateful country were rendered to all the officers, seamen, and Marines of the squadron.

In the latter part of 1747, *Admiral Boscawen* had sailed from England with a fleet of ships, and a number of Marines, and other forces, in order to reinforce the British fleet in the East Indies, with instructions to make an attack upon the *Island of Mauritius*, and subsequently to effect the conquest of *Pondicherry*, which was the chief object of the expedition.

After having reconnoitred the coast of the Mauritius, it was ascertained that the powerful means of defence everywhere presented, and the dangers in many places of approaching the land, would involve a great sacrifice of men, and render success ultimately doubtful; the coming on of the autumnal monsoons had also an influence in the decision of a council, which was to relinquish the attempt, and to proceed without delay for the *Coast of Coromandel*, according to the prescribed plan of operations.

About the end of June, 1748, the Admiral quitted 1748 the Coasts of the Mauritius, and proceeded to *Fort St. David,* where the troops were landed, and encamped with all the necessary stores; the Marines from four ships sent to Europe under Admiral Griffin, were added to the battalion employed on this service. The

1748 forces employed amounted to six thousand British and Native Auxiliary troops, and upwards of one thousand sailors, trained to the use of small arms, who were to form the besieging army. The battering cannon, mortars, and every implement were conveyed by the squadron within two miles of the town, while the land forces marched on the 8th of August towards *Pondicherry,* about thirty miles distant.

After several unsuccessful attempts, the troops crossed the river of *Arian Coupan,* and obtained possession of a strong situation within a mile of that Fort; a communication was maintained from thence with the fleet; and all the implements necessary for the siege were landed.

On the 25th of September the batteries were completed, and began to play; but, notwithstanding a combined cannonade on the part of the squadron against the town, it was found that the enemy's fire gained an ascendency over the besiegers. The fatigues endured by the troops, sickness becoming prevalent, and the rainy season being daily expected, which would inundate the country, and render retreat impracticable, afforded strong grounds, on which a Council of War, held on the 30th of September, determined to abandon the siege, to re-embark the men and stores, and to destroy the batteries. The troops fortunately reached Fort St. David on the evening of the 7th of October, after having demolished the fort of *Arian Coupan* on their way; the heavy rains which fell on the same evening had nearly rendered the rivers impassable.

On the 13th of February, 1748, the British squadron in the West Indies sailed from Jamaica under the command of Rear-Admiral Knowles, on an expedition against St. Jago, in Cuba, for which purpose some land-forces were embarked at Jamaica, and being joined 1748 with the Marines of the squadron, the whole put to sea; but after persevering for some time against strong northerly winds, which prevented their approaching that coast, the design was given up, and the force was directed against *Port Louis,* on the south side of Hispaniola, before which place it arrived on the 8th of March. The service was performed by the ships in line of battle, which, after three hours' heavy cannonade, compelled the governor, M. de Chaleaunoye, to surrender, when Major Scott, with a detachment of Colonel Trelawny's, the forty-ninth regiment, and the Marines, were landed, and took possession of the Fort in the name of His Majesty. After having shipped or destroyed upwards of eighty heavy cannon, and blown up the works, the whole were re-embarked; and Rear-Admiral Knowles resumed his former design against St. Jago, where he arrived on the 5th of April. The Plymouth and Cornwall were ordered to enter the harbour, but after firing a few broadsides at the castle, it was considered prudent to desist, and the squadron returned to Jamaica.

The distresses of France arising from the destruction of her Navy, and the annihilation of her commerce, compelled King Louis XV. to express a desire for peace. Accordingly, a congress was held at *Aix-la-Chapelle,* in order to negotiate the terms on which peace could be restored. The desire expressed by the King of France, as well as of Spain, did not, however, induce the British Government to relax in its efforts to reduce the means which those powers never failed to use, when opportunities offered, of thwarting the measures of Great Britain.

The negotiations, commenced at Aix-la-Chapelle in June, 1748, produced a Definitive Treaty of Peace,

46   FORMATION AND SERVICES OF MARINE CORPS.

1748 which was concluded on the 18th of October of that year, and was proclaimed on the 2nd of February, 1749.

Among the many reductions which took place during 1748, consequent on the General Peace, the Ten regiments of Marines were disbanded in November of that year, the officers of which were placed on half-pay.

1755   The conditions of the Peace concluded with France in 1748, were broken as soon as that Power had recovered from the effects of the former war: the interval of six years had been devoted to extending her Naval preparations, and to negotiations with other States, in order to reduce, or destroy, the power of Great Britain.

After enduring many insults, and witnessing the hostile measures which were preparing in the ports of France, the energies of the British nation were again aroused, and in the spring of 1755 considerable augmentations were made in the Army and Navy, and fifty companies of Marines were directed to be raised and placed under the control of the Lords Commissioners of the Admiralty. These companies were formed into three Divisions, and stationed at Chatham, Portsmouth, and Plymouth, and an Act of Parliament was passed for the "Regulation of the Marine forces while on shore."*

From the 5th of April, 1755, the Marine corps have constituted a branch of the permanent national force, and have been provided for in the annual votes of the House of Commons, on distinct estimates produced at each session, of the Navy, Army, and Marines.

War was declared against France on the 18th May in the following year (1756).

---

* A *Fourth* Division was added to the Establishment of the Royal Marines, by Order in Council dated 15th August, 1805, and stationed at Woolwich.

FORMATION AND SERVICES OF MARINE CORPS.

The foregoing pages contain accounts of the services of the *Corps of Marines* from the earliest period of their formation, to the year 1748, when they ceased to form a portion of the establishment of the Army. These historical details afford numerous instances in which the gallant exertions of the Marines have materially contributed to the successes obtained by the Navy and Army, and to the honours and advantages which have resulted from their combined operations.

1755

The services of the present Marine forces have been, as in former years, highly useful and efficient, and by their uniformly good conduct they have obtained the approbation of the Sovereign, and the confidence of the Country.

As a lasting mark of approbation, His Majesty King George III. was pleased, in 1802, to direct that they should be styled "*The Royal Marines*," as announced in the following Order, issued by the Lords Commissioners of the Admiralty, and inserted in the London Gazette, dated

1802

"*Admiralty Office*, 29th *April*, 1802.

"His Majesty has been graciously pleased to signify
"His Commands, that, in consideration of the very me-
"ritorious services of the Marines during the late War,
"the Corps shall in future be styled 'THE ROYAL
"'MARINES.'

"By Command of their Lordships.
    (Signed)   "EVAN NEPEAN."

On acquiring the title of *Royal*, the facings of the Marines, which had been *White*, were changed to *Blue*, as in other Royal corps of Infantry.*

---

* The LAUREL was authorised to be borne as a testimony of the gallantry of the Marines at the siege of Belle-Isle in the year 1761, and is encircled about the figure of the GLOBE on the Colours.

1827 On the 26th of September, 1827, New Colours were presented to the Division of Royal Marines at Chatham, on the part of His Majesty King George IV., by His Royal Highness the Duke of Clarence, then Lord High Admiral of Great Britain, and General of Marines, afterwards King William IV.

After alluding to the services of Marine regiments from the period of their formation to the present time, His Royal Highness caused the New Colours to be unfurled, and concluded his address in the following terms:

" His Majesty has selected for the Royal Marines
" *Device*, to which their achievements have entitled
" them, and which, by his permission, I this day pre-
" sented to you;—a *Badge* which you have so hardly
" and honorably earned:—From the difficulty of
" selecting any particular places to inscribe on these
" Standards, your Sovereign has been pleased to adopt
" ' *The Great Globe itself*,' as the most proper and
" distinctive badge. He has also directed, that
" his own name (*George IV.*) shall be added to that
" peculiar badge, THE ANCHOR, which is your distinctive
" bearing, in order that it may be known hereafter,
" that GEORGE THE FOURTH had conferred on you the
" honorable and well-earned badge this day presented
" to you.

" The motto, peculiarly your own, '*Per Mare; Per
" Terram*,' has been allowed to remain; and surmount-
" ing the entire is the word GIBRALTAR, in comme-
" moration of the important national services you per-
" formed there. In presenting these Colours, the gift
" of your Sovereign, into your hands, I trust,—I am
" confident,—you will defend them with the same in-
" trepidity, loyalty, and regard for the interests of the
" country, that have marked your preservation of your
" old ones; and if you do, your Sovereign, and your
" Country, will have equal reason to be satisfied."

THE
ROYAL MARINES

For Cannon's Military Records

(49)

APPENDIX TO THE MARINE CORPS.

THE following memoranda are appended to this narrative of the services of the Royal Marines, in order to show the relative positions in which the Marine regiments were placed, in respect to *rank and precedence*, with the regiments of Infantry, during the period the Marine regiments were borne on the establishment of the regular army, and the ground on which the present corps of Royal Marines have been authorised, when acting with the infantry of the line, to take their station next to the *Forty-ninth* regiment, according to the date of their formation in the year 1755, as shown in the following pages.

The rank of the several regiments of the British army was first regulated by a Board of General Officers assembled in the Netherlands, by command of King William III., on the 10th June, 1694.

Another Board of General Officers was assembled by order of Queen Anne, in 1713, to decide on the rank and precedence of regiments raised subsequently to 1694.

A third Board was assembled, by command of King George I., in 1715, for the same purpose.

These Boards recommended that English regiments raised in England, should take rank from the dates of their formation, and that English, Scots, and Irish regiments, raised for the service of a foreign power, should take rank from the dates of their being placed on the English establishment.

The *Numerical Titles* of regiments, as fixed on the principle laid down in the reports of the Boards of General Officers, above alluded to, were confirmed by the warrant issued by authority of King George II., dated 1st July, 1751, —and also by the warrant of King George III., dated 19th December, 1768, previously to which periods regiments were generally designated by the names of their Colonels.

1. The principle on which the Numerical Titles of regiments were fixed, having been thus established by Royal authority, the regiments of infantry which had been formed

E

by King Charles II., on his Restoration to the Throne in 1660, and those which had been subsequently raised in the reigns of King James II. and of William III., were numbered according to the dates of being placed on the English establishment, —from the *First, or Royal,* regiment to the *Twenty-seventh* regiment.

2. The regiments of infantry, which had been added to the army in the reign of Queen Anne from the year 1702, and retained on the establishment after the Peace of Utrecht in 1713, commenced with the *Twenty-eighth,* and ended with the *Thirty-ninth* regiment.

3. The *Fortieth* regiment was formed in the year 1717, from independent companies in North America and the West Indies:—the command was conferred on Colonel Richard Philips.

4. The *Forty-first* regiment was formed from Invalids in 1719:—the command was conferred on Colonel Edmund Fielding.

5. The other regiments of infantry, raised by King George I. on the augmentation of the army in the year 1715, were disbanded in 1718, after the Monarchy, in the line of the House of Brunswick, had been established, and the Peace of the Kingdom restored.

6. The *Forty-second Highland* regiment was formed in the reign of King George II. from independent companies in Scotland, in the year 1739. It was originally termed " *The Black Watch,*" and was placed on the establishment on the 25th October, 1739:—the command was conferred on Colonel James Earl of Crawford.*

7. The *Forty-third* regiment was raised for service in America, in the year 1740, by Colonel Andrew Spotswood, and afterwards commanded by Colonel W. Gooche. It was disbanded in 1743.

---

* The Corps, which had been formed in 1737 by Colonel James Oglethorpe for service in Georgia and South Carolina, was disbanded in 1749. It had not been ranked in the number of regiments of infantry in the Official Records of the Army, although in some publications of that period it was numbered the *Forty-second* regiment, according to its seniority and the date of its formation.

APPENDIX TO THE MARINE CORPS. 51

8. The Ten regiments of Marines raised in 1739 and 1740, were numbered from the 44th to the 53rd regiments, as shown in the following list, viz. :—

Marine Regiments.	Names of the Colonels.	Periods of Formation, &c.	Colour of the Facing.	Precedence in the Regiments of Infantry of the Line.
1st Regiment	E. Wolfe	1739	Deep Yellow	44th Foot.
,, ,,	G. Keightley	1745		
,, ,,	G. Churchill	1745		
2nd Regiment	Wm. Robinson	1739	Green	45th Foot.
,, ,,	Rt. Frazer	1741		
3rd Regiment	Anthony Lowther.	1739	Light Yellow	46th Foot.
,, ,,	R. Sowle	1745		
,, ,,	H. Holmes	1746		
4th Regiment	J. Wynyard	1739	White	47th Foot.
,, ,,	Jas. Long	1742		
,, ,,	Byng, afterwards Visct. Torrington	1744		
5th Regiment	C. Douglas	1739	Primrose Yellow	48th Foot.
,, ,,	J. Grant	1741		
,, ,,	S. Daniel	1741		
,, ,,	Jas. Cochrane	1741		
6th Regiment	Honble. Lucius Ducie Moreton	1739	Green Cuffs, Collar, and Cap	49th Foot.
,, ,,	J. Cotterell	1741		
,, ,,	Honble. W. Herbert	1747		
,, ,,	Jas. Laforey	1747		
7th Regiment	H. Cornwall	1740	White	50th Foot.
8th Regiment	W. Hanmore	1740	Light Yellow	51st Foot.
,, ,,	J. Duncombe	1742		
,, ,,	Lord G. Beauclerk	1747		
,, ,,	Jas. Jordan	1748		
9th Regiment	C. Powlett	1740	Buff	52nd Foot.
10th Regiment	J. Jeffreys	1740	Deep Yellow	53rd Foot.
,, ,,	Sir Andrew Agnew	1746		

The above ten regiments were disbanded in November, 1748.

9. The following seven regiments were raised, and added to the establishment of the army, in January, 1741; and in consequence of the disbandment of Colonel Spotswood's, afterwards Gooche's, American Provincials, and also of the ten regiments of Marines, the *numerical* titles of six of these regiments were changed, after the peace of 1748, as specified in the following list; viz.:—

54th Regt., com. by Colonel Thomas Fowke, now the 43rd Regt.
55th   „   „   „   James Long, . „   44th Regt.
56th   „   „   „   D. Houghton, . „   45th Regt.
57th   „   „   „   James Price, . „   46th Regt.
58th   „   „   „   J. Mordaunt, . „   47th Regt.
59th   „   „   „   J. Cholmondeley,   „   48th Regt.
60th   „   „   H. De Grangue, disbanded in 1748.

10. The *Forty-ninth* regiment was formed in the year 1743, of two companies of one of the regiments raised in the reign of Queen Anne, which had remained at Jamaica, and of six other companies formed in that colony. The command was given to Colonel Edward Trelawny, then Governor of Jamaica. It was retained on the establishment after the peace of 1748, and numbered the 49th regiment.

11. On the recommencement of hostilities with France in 1755, fifty companies of Marines were raised, under the direction and control of the Lords Commissioners of the Admiralty. These companies were formed into *three divisions*, at the principal naval stations, Portsmouth, Plymouth, and Chatham.* The *Corps of Marines* having been raised in 1755, and since that period retained on the establishment, as a branch of the permanent national force of Navy, Army, and Marines, have been authorised to rank, when acting with infantry of the line, *next to the Forty-ninth Regiment*, as directed by His Majesty King George IV. in the following General Order, dated

"*Horse-Guards*, 30*th March*, 1820.

"In reference to the *Regulations regarding Precedence* "*of Regiments* (as contained in page 10 of the General "Regulations and Orders of the Army), His Majesty has been "graciously pleased to command, that the *Royal Marines*, "when acting with the Troops of the Line, shall take their "station next to the Forty-ninth Regiment.

"By Command of H. R. H. the Commander-in-Chief.

"Henry Torrens, *Adjutant-General*."

---

* A *Fourth Division* was formed at Woolwich by Order in Council dated 15th August, 1805.

APPENDIX TO THE MARINE CORPS. 53

12. In the year 1745 two regiments were raised for service in North America, by Colonel William Shirley and Colonel Sir William Pepperell. In 1754 they were numbered the 50th and 51st Regiments.

13. In December, 1755, eleven regiments were raised and added to the establishment of the army; and in consequence of the disbandment of Colonel Shirley's and Sir William Pepperell's regiments in 1757, the eleven regiments, above alluded to, were ranked two numbers higher in the list of regiments of infantry, as shown in the following list; viz. :—

52nd Regt., com. by Colonel James Abercromby now the 50th Regt.
53rd   „   „   Robt. Napier,   .   „   51st Regt.
54th   „   „   H. Lambton,   . .   „   52nd Regt.
55th   „   „   W. Whitmore,   .   „   53rd Regt.
56th   „   „   John Campbell, .   „   54th Regt.
57th   „   „   G. Perry . . .   „   55th Regt.
58th   „   „   Lord C. Manners .   „   56th Regt.
59th   „   „   John Arabin . .   „   57th Regt.
60th   „   „   Robt. Anstruther .   „   58th Regt.
61st   „   „   Charles Montagu .   „   59th Regt.
62nd Royal American,}
  of *four* battalions,} Col. The Earl of Loudon, „   60th Regt.

14. In April, 1758, the *Second Battalions* of the fifteen regiments, undermentioned, were formed into distinct regiments, and numbered as shown in the following list; viz. :—

3rd Foot, 2d Batt., const^d 61st Regt. | 19th Foot, 2d Batt., const^d 66th Regt.
4th Foot,   „   „   62nd Regt. | 20th Foot,   „   „   67th Regt.
8th Foot,   „   „   63rd Regt. | 23rd Foot,   „   „   68th Regt.
11th Foot, „   „   64th Regt. | 24th Foot,   „   „   69th Regt.
12th Foot, „   „   65th Regt. | 31st Foot,   „   „   70th Regt.

The Second Battalion of the 32nd was constituted the 71st Regt.
       „   „   33rd   „   :,   72nd Regt.
       „   „   34th   „   ,,   73rd Regt.
       „   „   36th   „   ,,   74th Regt.
       „   „   37th   „   ,,   75th Regt.

After the peace of Fontainebleau, in 1763, reductions were made in the regular army, and the number of regiments of infantry was limited to SEVENTY. The above 71st, 72nd, 73rd, 74th, and 75th Regiments were consequently disbanded in that year.

15. The number of regiments of infantry continued at *Seventy*, until the commencement of the American War in

1775, and the renewal of hostilities with France and Spain in 1779, when it was increased to *One hundred and Five* regiments, exclusive of *Eleven* unnumbered regiments, and thirty-six independent companies of Invalids.

16. After the General Peace in 1782 the number of regiments of infantry was again reduced.

17. In consequence of an increase of possessions in India, and of additional troops being necessary for the suppression of certain native powers, which were hostile to the British Government, additional corps were raised and embarked for the East Indies in 1779, and in subsequent years.

18. The present *Seventy-first* regiment was raised in December, 1777, and embarked for India in 1779. Its number was changed from 73rd to 71st regiment in 1786.

19. The present *Seventy-second* regiment was raised in December, 1777, and embarked for India in 1781. Its number was changed from 78th to 72nd regiment in 1786.

20. The *Seventy-third* regiment was raised as the second battalion of the Forty-second (Highland) regiment in 1777, and embarked for India in 1781. It was formed into a distinct regiment, and numbered the 73rd (Highland) in 1786.

21. The 74th (Highland), 75th (Highland), 76th, and 77th regiments were raised for service in India in October, 1787, and embarked for India in 1788.

22. The 78th (Highland), 79th (Highland), 80th, 81st, 82nd, 83rd, 84th, 85th, 86th, 87th, 88th, 89th, 90th, and 91st (Highland) regiments were raised in 1793, immediately after the commencement of the war with France, occasioned by the revolutionary and violent proceedings in that country in 1793.

23. The 92nd (Highland) and 93rd (Highland) regiments were raised and placed on the establishment of the army, the former on the 3rd May, 1796, and the latter on the 25th August, 1800.

24. The *Scots Brigade* was numbered the *Ninety-fourth* regiment on the 25th December, 1802. This corps had been formed in the year 1568, for service in Holland against the

APPENDIX TO THE MARINE CORPS. 55

oppression of Spain. Being a British corps, its services were demanded from the United Provinces by King James II. on the rebellion of the Duke of Monmouth in 1685, after the suppression of which it returned to Holland. It again embarked for England with the Prince of Orange at the Revolution in 1688. It remained in Great Britain until the Protestant cause had been established, and it re-embarked for Flanders in 1691, and served in the campaigns of King William III. It remained in the service of Holland until 1793, when it was decided by King George III., upon the application of the British officers remaining in it, to require the corps to return to Great Britain. It was taken on the British Establishment on the 5th July, 1793. It then consisted of *Three* battalions; in 1795 it was reduced to *Two* battalions, and embarked for Gibraltar. In 1796 it was formed into *One* battalion, and proceeded to the Cape of Good Hope. It embarked, in 1798, for the East Indies, from whence, after much distinguished service, it returned to England in 1808. It embarked for Cadiz and Lisbon, and served with great credit in the Peninsular War, from January, 1810, to July, 1814. It was disbanded at Belfast on the 24th December, 1818.

25. The *Rifle Corps*, commanded by Colonel Coote Manningham, was formed and added to the establishment of the Army on the 25th August, 1800. On 25th December, 1802, it was directed to be numbered the *Ninety-fifth* regiment, but was taken out of the list of *numbered* regiments of infantry on the 6th February, 1816, and directed to be styled " *The Rifle Brigade.*" It then consisted of three battalions, which were distributed at the following stations, viz. :—

1st Battalion.—6 Companies with the Army of Occupation in France, and 4 Companies at Shorncliffe.
2nd Battalion.—6 Companies with the Army of Occupation in France, and 4 Companies at Shorncliffe.
3rd Battalion.—10 Companies at Dover. This Battalion embarked for Ireland in March, 1816. It was disbanded at Birr on the 24th of November, 1818.

26. The present 94th, 95th, 96th, 97th, 98th, and 99th regiments were added to the establishment of the Army in the early part of the year 1824, in consequence of the increased number of the colonial possessions of the British Empire.

Note.—The Compiler of these Records feels it a duty to acknowledge, that he has derived a principal portion of the means of drawing up the details of the services of the Marines from " *An Historical Review of the Royal Marine Corps,*" *published in* 1803, " *by Captain Alexander Gillespie, who served as an Officer in that Corps upwards of twenty-four years;*" a work of considerable merit and research, which reflects great honor on its author, as an excellent scholar and a most zealous officer.

www.ingramcontent.com/pod-product-compliance
Lightning Source LLC
Chambersburg PA
CBHW020020050426
42450CB00005B/567